A CHANGE IN THE AIR

Jane Clarke was born in 1961 and grew up on a farm in Co. Roscommon. She lives with her wife in Glenmalure, Co. Wicklow, where she combines writing with her work as a creative writing tutor. She holds a BA in English and Philosophy from Trinity College, Dublin, and an MPhil in Writing from the University of South Wales, and has a background in psychoanalytic psychotherapy.

Her first collection, *The River*, was published by Bloodaxe Books in 2015. It was shortlisted for the Royal Society of Literature's Ondaatje Prize, given for a distinguished work of fiction, non-fiction or poetry evoking the spirit of a place. In 2016 she won the Hennessy Literary Award for Emerging Poetry and the inaugural Listowel Writers' Week Poem of the Year Award. Jane was awarded Arts Council of Ireland Literary Bursaries in 2017 and 2021. She received the Ireland Chair of Poetry Travel Award 2022.

Her second collection, *When the Tree Falls*, was published by Bloodaxe Books in 2019. It was shortlisted for the Pigott Poetry Prize 2020, the *Irish Times* Poetry Now Award 2020 and the Farmgate Café National Poetry Award 2020 as well as being longlisted for the Royal Society for Literature Ondaatje Award 2020. 'Copper Soles' from *When the Tree Falls* was highly commended in the Forward Book of Poetry 2021.

All the Way Home, Jane's illustrated booklet of poems written in response to a First World War family archive held in the Mary Evans Picture Library, London, was published by Smith | Doorstop in 2019. Her third book-length collection, A *Change in the Air*, was published by Bloodaxe Books in 2023.

Jane also edited *Origami Doll: New and Collected Shirley McClure* (Arlen House, 2019), and guest-edited *The North 61: Irish Issue* (The Poetry Business, 2019) with Nessa O'Mahony.

www.janeclarkepoetry.ie

JANE CLARKE

A Change in the Air

BLOODAXE BOOKS

ISBN: 978 1 78037 659 2

First published 2023 by
Bloodaxe Books Ltd,
Eastburn,
South Park,
Hexham,
Northumberland NE46 1BS

www.bloodaxebooks.com
For further information about Bloodaxe titles
please visit our website and join our mailing list
or write to the above address for a catalogue.

Cover design: Neil Astley & Pamela Robertson-Pearce.

Printed in Great Britain by Bell & Bain Limited, Glasgow, Scotland, on
acid-free paper sourced from mills with FSC chain of custody certification.

For Isobel

CONTENTS

After

Now that her heart is bent over
like larkspur after a storm,

she stays in bed past milking time,
pulling the quilt

tight around her shoulders
until her collie barks her

down the stairs
to lift the backdoor latch.

She kneels to light the cipeens
piled on last night's embers.

Her bones creak
like the bolt on the door of the barn.

A cup of oats, two cups of water,
a pinch of salt –

porridge, tea and tablets,
a meal for a queen.

Every day without him
is too long;

she's waiting
with the tired cows at the gate.

Butter for Queens

My mother craves new potatoes –
dripping with butter, sprinkled with salt.

They taste of the earth, she says
and remind her of corncrake mornings,
crex crex   crex crex from the fields.

She'd skim the cream,
let it sit on the sill to ripen,

hold the jug high and pour,
then turn and turn to a rhythm
unhurried as milking,

till the butter balls clustered,
floating yellow as freshly dug Queens.

In her days of gathering dusk,
she clasps them under the pump,
rinses till the water runs clean.

Raspberries

Sunday morning stillness
in a thicket of canes –

my mother reaches
for quilted berries,

eases them red and willing
from yellow stalks,

ready to hull
for the simmering.

She tells me
not to forget

a pound of sugar
for every pound of fruit,

says I must remember
because something

has slipped into her mind
and every night,

like a stoat among voles,
it hunts down her memories.

District Nurse

Nurse Murray cycled from beyond Ballinleg
        to help her latch the firstborn to her breast.

She rolled a pebble, small as a baby's tummy,
        so my mother could see she was giving him plenty.

Today's nurse asks about her memory
        and holds up pictures of brain cells.

I query the *ifs* and *whens*
        while my mother listens as if to the leaves

that crinkle and rust on her favourite tree.
        She recalls Nurse Brehony from Oran,

who nursed her father when he was dying,
        which he did as gently as he did everything else.

The farmyard's grey as the roof slates.
        Leaning against her car, the nurse tells me

her mother's loss was gradual. The horse chestnut gives us shelter
        from drizzle that brings a million drops of rain.

Dressing My Mother for Her Grandson's Wedding

A darker shade of blue than her eyes,
the dress has slept for years in the wardrobe

next to the clothes she won't let me give away.
She raises her arms for me, though she's forgotten

why she can't stay by the fire with her collie.
A new pair of tights. An old pair of shoes,

softened at the toes and heels.
She winces at the touch of the hairbrush.

No sign of her pearls.
I dredge through photos and medicines

on top of the chest of drawers,
find them coiled around her engagement ring.

She chooses a scarf, red as her lipstick.
I tell her there's a beautiful woman in the mirror –

she laughs,
I might find a new man at the wedding,

and then in a whisper, *Sorry Charlie*
as if he's with us in their bedroom, listening.

Given

At a market stall on Bantry square
the woman in a blue-striped apron

tells me yoghurt making's a mystery,
no two batches taste the same.

Try as she might for consistency,
she's surprised by the flavours

from barely acidic to bitter as sloes,
textures thicker than buttermilk,

thinner than consommé.
She questions everything; the milk,

the starter culture, the heat of fermentation.
On a good day she savours the difference,

the way a mother might look at her children,
in wonder at what she's been given.

Becoming

(after Lorna Goodison)

I am becoming mother
to my mother; closer

to mother than I have ever
been. I feed, bathe

and console my mother
who fed, bathed and consoled me.

I read my mother stories
till she falls asleep

to dream of her mother
coming to take her from me.

All the horses she's ever loved

gather round my mother's bed —
Bess from Abergavenny would leap any fence
for the company of cows; Fred would let himself

out of the stable and lift his headcollar off the peg;
Rory stomped into the kitchen one evening
and devoured a loaf of oven-warm bread.

Only yesterday she and her sisters
were in the trap on the way to school
with the pony that yearned to race the train.

He galloped the long bog road
from Ballymoe and not even her father,
holding the reins, could slow him.

Now Sunday morning, she's with her brother
in the haggard pitching hay from a rick;
before the church bell rings in the village

the cattle must be fed. They build the load,
tie it with ropes and heel up the shafts
to back in the Clydesdale by the bridle.

At first she frets about steering Jack
as he pulls the cart, swaying up the narrow lane
and through the gateway,

But horses have more gumption
than any of us, she says.
She loosens the reins, gives him his head.

Eggs

I'd have followed her anywhere
but my grandmother rarely went farther
than the yard, tending her hens.

Every morning she poured fresh water
and ladled corn into the dented tin dish,
adding handfuls of seeds and grit.

From a gap in the galvanised roof
the sun lit the lines on her face.
She'd let me reach into nest boxes

to grasp warm eggs, then slip them
into her cardigan pockets. She chased
the cantankerous cockerel away

and warned, *Watch out for men
who fancy themselves*. At the kitchen table
we'd divvy up the eggs, roll

the surplus in melted lard and salt
and stow them in the scullery,
like pullets roosting on a high shelf.

All she needed

Days when bronchitis wheezed
like a plibín in her chest, she lit

the fire early. I leaned back
against her knees, my cheeks red

as the turf flames. She helped me
loop wool around needles for plain

and purl and sounded out the shapes
beneath the pictures in my book –

hens and eggs, cats and kittens,
milk and bread. Granny left school

to wash and cook for her father
and brothers, *I'd learned all I needed*

by the time I was twelve.
She never mentioned her mother's name,

age or homeplace,
only that she died in childbirth,

as if it was as natural as losing a ewe
on a cold winter's night.

Milk

Tall as my hip, the gentlest creature
I've ever met, she waits by the manger

while I, on a three-legged stool,
tuck myself close to her belly,

my legs hugging the bucket tight.
I hold each teat between thumb

and first finger, then squeeze –
it takes time to find the rhythm

that lets the milk flow. Meanwhile
this Jersey stands still as Lough Glinn,

her warm teats filling my hands,
that have been so empty and cold.

The Lookout

Through wind and rain he lay in wait,
an hour or more on the garden wall,

till he spotted the yellow school bus
at the top of the road.

When he heard us laughing,
shouting, squabbling,

he jumped barking to the gravel
and ran to gather his flock of five.

The evening he arrived in the kitchen
(the runt from our uncle's best collie),

he peed on the tiles,
but never again till near the end

when his legs wouldn't carry him
to the back door – long after he'd taught us

all he knew about love that waits
in the wind and rain.

The Arch

Not Tudor or corbel,
lancet or Gothic,

not burdened by a bridge
or chastened by a church,

but hewn from rough limestone blocks,
wedged flank to flank by peasant masons,

it stands at the end of the avenue
in chestnut-tree shade.

It has sent off scoundrels,
barred bailiffs from entry,

welcomed carriages home.
It never sleeps on duty,

never refuses swallows a nest,
never tells stories better unsaid.

Years it watched the courtyard walls
crumble and fall, till it was left alone.

When will it stop trying to hold
what can no longer be held?

PIT PONIES OF GLENDASAN

Christmas Morning

Washed clean as ore in a buddle,
the miners hold lanterns high
to guide them down the glen.

Sore heads crave peace
after a night in the sheebeen,
black eyes and bruises

from fist fights at the brothel door.
Tumbling down from Camenabologue,
the Avonbeg river keeps pace

with their homesick stride.
Like copper and zinc at the jig table,
the men divide at Greenane Bridge,

for Latin Mass in St. Columba's,
Morning Prayer at Ballinatone.
They belt out carols they learned

as children, listen to the story of hope,
then kneel to petition for clear lungs,
safe shifts and the price of lead to hold.

Pit Ponies of Glendasan

Hitched to an eight-hour shift
in britchens, hames and traces,

they follow the miners' carbide lights,
halt under hoppers, turn

on a thruppence and lean into their collars
to pull the five-wagon train.

Low-set cobs from the Curragh,
a piebald and two greys, their hooves

fall heavy as hammers on granite.
They haul lengths of larch for pit props,

pneumatic drills, boxes of gelignite,
and, from time to time, deliver

injured men back to daylight.
The miners pat their necks in passing

and feed them windfall apples –
comrades in toil and first to halt,

legs locked at a sudden rumbling, a change
in the air or the rush of running water.

The Pay

I'd like to tell you I felt no fear
but every hour under Camaderry

      was an hour too close to rockfall –
      jackhammer pounding, dynamite roar –

seven feet high, four feet wide,
the tunnel mapped the mineral seam.

      My brothers quit for better pay,
      digging drains in Camden.

But the mountains wouldn't let me go.
Frost an inch thick on my shovel,

      I filled wagons with granite and lead,
      muscled them out of the tunnel

to tip into the crusher,
the master who had to be fed.

      Now brambles wreathe the adits,
      moss smooths broken stone.

I'm hard of hearing, half-crippled,
hands fissured as schist

      and still, my heart lifts to see
      morning mist veiling Tonelagee.

Mullacor

(for Robbie Carter)

Two miners lead two mules up a winding track
past the Smelting House and Ballinafunshoge adit –

hobnailed boots and iron-shod hooves grind
pine needles into granite. Halfway up they stop

to drink from the stream that rings silver
through gorse and fraughan to the Mill Brook waterwheel.

The mules lengthen their stride at the pass, unflinching
when whimbrel careen from cotton grass,

calls rippling across the heath. At the edge of the cutting
the men bend and heave to fill the creels with footed peat.

Above them, forked tail and finger-tipped wings,
a lone red kite drifts bronze as withered bracken.

ALL THE WAY HOME

September 1914

The week before he left for France
we leaned a ladder into the apple trees,

picked Cox's Orange Pippins,
Newton Wonders, Brownlee's Russets,

laid them one by one
on dusty floorboards in the attic,

then planted hyacinths and amaryllis for spring.
We sat out after dinner

and talked of how we loved
this time of year,

when hollyhocks are past their best
but still stand tall

in copper, pink and cream,
beside clematis and the last of the sweet pea.

In the dugout

To pass the time in the dugout, they play
the 'when all this is over' game.

In the beginning their plans were bold,
one chap keen to outdo the next.

Now it's *a drink in the local,*
Sunday dinner with all the trimmings,

to walk in the Malverns,
waltz with my wife in the kitchen,

hold my mother's hand,
watch my children sleep,

wishes distilled to the final drop
like Scotch in a copper still.

The Game

From an eyewitness account by Fr Browne,
chaplain to the Irish Guards, 1916–1920

The goal posts were blown
to matchsticks –

seven men wounded,
two defenders
and a keeper dead.

Still hot,
their bodies were stretchered
from the pitch.

Friends filled their places.
The referee blew the whistle again.

After we're gone

farmers will level the ground,
backfilling shell-holes and trenches,

picking coins, buttons, tin cups,
boot laces, shaving mugs, razors

from soil that has buried letters,
curses, men and horses.

They'll never know one of the lads
keeps celandine and meadowsweet

in a whiskey glass by his pallet,
another passes the time at the parapet

naming the flowers in his mother's garden:
foxgloves, peonies, lupins, heart's ease.

When I try to forget what I've seen
I think of my neighbours

with rakes and scythes between hedges
scented by honeysuckle and wild rose.

Bouchavesnes

Some men sing, some men chat,
all complain about the heat;

they've been digging since early,
another twenty graves.

While they bend and lift,
wielding pickaxe, mattock, spade,

a soldier thinks of his grandad
digging potatoes –

wait till the vines have died down,
he'd say, be sure to dig gently

or you'll bruise the tubers that huddle
like hens' eggs under the mound.

Then let your shovel lift
seven, eight, nine, into the light.

Priam of Troy

Poor as a peddler
        in a mule-drawn cart,
                he leaves his city at night –

bound for the camp
        across the plain,
                carrying gifts; the finest tunics,

robes, blankets, cloaks,
        woven from wool
                of young sheep and goats,

woven to warm,
        comfort, bind
                what is broken.

Ling

A sprig of heather falling
from his sister's letter

carries him home
to the slopes of Slieve Donard –

a sea of honey-scented ling,
purple flowers teeming with bees.

A shepherd told them
that at the time of creation

no plant would cover
the bare mountain slopes;

only heather, out of kindness,
offered its modest growth.

A brave little plant, he called it.
No matter how trampled

by rutting stags,
the woody branches always spring back.

When all this is over

we'll follow a path
>   through silver birch and pine

listen for the shepherd
>   whistling to her flock of pregnant ewes

look for grasses
>   herbs trampled under their hooves

catch the scent
>   of crushed chamomile lavender thyme

from the mossy mountainside
>   drink the river's source

It will all be over one day, and what a day it will be, won't it?
Albert Auerbach (1894–1918) in a letter from the trenches to his sister in London.

Snow

began to fall before dawn,
blown horizontal in easterly winds

from across the hill. By evening
it lies deep in banks and drifts;

hedges become whitewashed walls,
barrels turn into haystacks,

the wood pile disappears.
She could almost believe

that they haven't received
his mud-caked kit, breeches ripped

from ankle to hip, bloodied tunic,
his helmet, slightly dinged,

and the watch he won at school.
She could believe he'll be with them

for dinner, having walked in his trench boots,
all the way home through the snow.

Pianist

she plays
into silence

a harbour
at dusk

makes wind-ripples
over the surface

hail stones
on the slipway

she dives
like a cormorant dives

leaves only
a circle of bubbles

we listen
for where she'll emerge

turning
her sleek black head

taking
our breath

she dives
again and again

returns us
to quietness

YOU COULD SAY IT BEGINS

You could say it begins

where a rill meets Lough Foyle
between Donegal and Derry,
then wends upstream to Liberty Bridge,
leans south-west, bends north-east,
skirts low hills and rambles across
the Skeoge valley to Bridgend,

rises to the summit of Holywell Hill,
down Liberty Burn to Kildrum and Killea,
strolls over to Drumnasheer, dips into
the Foyle as far as the bridge between
the twins, Lifford and Strabane, hems
the Finn south-west, close to Clady Bridge,

turns south to Fern Hill and ambles west
across windswept uplands, rolls into
the Mourne Beg until Sturagave Bridge,
south with the Sruhangarve, Glendergan,
Leaghany through forests to Carymouth
where the Derg flows into Lough Derg,

veers upstream along the Owenboy Burn,
runs through hillsides yellow with furze,
down to the Termon through Pettigo town
and into Lough Erne with mayfly and trout,
west along the Waterfort to Lough Awaddy,
Lough Rushen and Lough Vearty,

slips south to Keenaghan Lough, westward again
to the River Erne, onwards to Bradoge Bridge,
west of Belleek, uphill with one stream,
downhill with the next to Abhornaleha Bridge,
south-east to where the County River
drops into Lough Melvin and along the valley

between Leitrim and Fermanagh, curves
east of Kiltyclogher, through Dean's Lough
where the Brent geese rest, trails the Black River
to the head of Lough Macneen Upper,
crosses the lake to the Belcoo River mouth,
climbs up and onto Cuilcagh ridge

where meadow pipits sing, races down
the easterly flank, then saunters north
past Swanlinbar, to the lee of Slieve Rusden,
traces the Woodford north-east past Ballyconnell,
through Lough Erne's rivulets north of Belturbet,
where it meets, then leaves the River Finn,

clambers uphill between Cavan and Fermanagh,
to Clontaty Bridge near Clones, back and forth
across the road to Lackey Bridge, roams north
to Roslea, back to the Finn and wooded foothills,
onto Sliabh Beagh, north-east through lake and stream,
across Lough More, descends west of Aughnacloy

into Blackwater valley between Monaghan
and Tyrone, cross-country to the River Cor, north
of Mullyash Mountain, follows the County Water
into the River Clarebane, plunges into Lough Ross,
west of Crossmaglen, and with the River Fane
laps Monaghan, Louth and Armagh,

winds through lowlands to the Flurry Bridge
and onwards with the Flurry, rounds the foothills
and shins up the summit of Clermont Mountain,
falls to the County Bridge and through the mouth
of the River Newry into the sea at Carlingford Lough
where you could say it ends, or maybe it begins.

Crossings

a gap in a hawthorn hedge   stepping stones in a stream

an oak log slick with frost   a three-arch masonry bridge

a cow path down to a river   where boulders span the width

a space between two barbed-wire strands   a five bar gate

a bye-road   a railway line   a deer run

a coffin path   a stile in a dry stone wall   a pass between two peaks

a row boat on a lake   a bramble-laced bridle path

a firebreak through conifers   a granite-lintelled sheep creep

a butter path   a footbridge over a burn

two breeze blocks and a plank   railway sleepers laid in a bog

Flight

Shove over the bolt, douse the lamps,
lie down on the kitchen floor,

her quiet father shouted
when he saw five men march
through the farmyard to the door.

He knew them from the fairs;
they'd chat about the weather,
the price of weanlings and heifers.

Let them not set the house alight,
her mother wept.

They don't want to harm us,
only to warn us,

her father shushed as bullets split
the shutters, splintered mirrors,
lodged in whitewashed walls.

They lay on the flagstones till dawn,
curled into each other; a smidgeon
of warmth from the stove.

Next day, neighbours helped them
empty the house and load two carts;
clothes thrown into baskets,

mattresses, blankets, rugs, cups and saucers
wrapped in tea towels, a can of milk,
gifts of cabbage and soda bread.

Sure you'll be back, they said,
when these troubles are settled.

Her father checked the harness, lifted her
up between her sisters, and tucked them in
with a blanket, the family bible at their feet.

Family Bible

Though the clasp is broken, flysheet
missing, frontispiece ripped,

my great-aunt's pressed violets survive
between the gilt-edged pages.

She underlined her favourite verses,
filled the endpapers with the births,

marriages, deaths of seven generations.
Tucked in for safe keeping:

a seed catalogue, a crumpled recipe
for Christmas cake and her sister's letters

from the border farm she married into.
Ruth sent news of selling vegetables and eggs

in Enniskillen market, holidays
at Malin Head, and then,

watch towers, cratered roads,
meadows trampled by foot patrols.

She wrote about silence among neighbours,
spreading stealthy as hoar frost,

but also kindness –
when a child is ill,

a harvest fails or a well runs dry,
we set our differences aside.

When the sun

rises beyond Cuilcagh's
gritstone ridge

let's tend
a sheltered acre

plant yarrow
to staunch the bleeding

vervain
to calm the fevers

comfrey
for broken bones

and for our sadness
borage and rose.

The Dipper

An Gabha Dubh

You fly upstream while I tramp

       among snow-dusted rushes
       along the suckering edge.

True as a mandrel

       you dive, flickering
       into the narrow rill.

I think I've lost you –

       but beyond clumps of sedge
       and withered asphodel,

little blacksmith,

       you bob on an anvil.
       Droplets fall from your bib.

Hammer to chisel,

       you hurtle notes
       higher and higher

above the river,

       your treble bell
       pealing across the heath.

Lazy Beds

In the shelter of Fancy Mountain,
        a man and woman rented
                an acre of rocky soil.

Peregrine falcons soared
        from their nests in the cliffs
                while the couple gleaned stones

for a two-room hut
        and a goat pen.
                They sliced through roots

of black bog rush and deer sedge,
        dug into peat, cutting
                and turning

sod onto sod.
        They planted potatoes
                when stonechats

clashed pebbles into song.
        The ridges resisted frost,
                held flinders of heat.

After the famine
        the valley was cleared for sheep,
                tenants shipped to Gross Île.

Ewes still graze the heath,
        rain still ripples
                down the furrows they built

and once in a while
        wind whips water into twisters
                that dance the width of Lough Tay.

skein

lifted on southerlies
from sloblands and bogs

louder and louder
until they're above us

yodeling and yelping
laughing or weeping

Passage

When are we leaving, who'll come
with us, how'll we get to the ship?

My scrawl of a girl has me mithered
with questions. *Whisht*, I tell her,

we must gather nettles and dock,
then search for blackbirds' eggs.

She's quiet awhile till she whispers,
Ye were crying last night.

Please God she hasn't heard talk
of the fever that haunts the ships.

She's seen mothers cradle babies
to the graveyard, men bent double

with corpses tied to their backs.
I'll lull her to sleep with tales

of soft feather beds in Quebec
and loaves of fresh-baked bread.

Her father will cross the ocean
to find us and he'll see her blossom

like the whitethorn
that brightens our byroad today.

Wildfire

Fire leaps from heath to trees –
      flames raze alder, oak and hazel,

routing hares from Purple Mountain,
      merlin out of bell and ling.

Smoke chokes herds of red and sika,
      vixens thread blazing gorse

to haul their cubs from dens.
      Squirrels scoot up higher,

chiffchaff, robins, goldcrests
      dropping light as twigs.

Pipistrelles and lesser horseshoes
      shrivel as they fly.

Night sky glows inferno red.
      nests, feathers, flesh –

a forest falling,
      ash on ash.

Rowan

When grief
like a river

is set
to burst its banks

the rowan
has already lost

its berries
and leaves;

it sways
in the wind,

steadies,
sways.

Refuge

a filly tracks her mother
> on the far side of the river

splashing and scrabbling
> through rocks along the edge

at a moss-mantled boulder
> impervious as a border post

the mare turns
> into the current

water swirls
> around her belly

churns high as her withers
> the Avonmore in spate

unwavering she trains her eyes
> on the other side

a clearing among hazel and birch
> flecked yellow with celandines

the foal traces her mother's steps –
> when the river reaches her breast

she raises her long and lovely head
> supple as willow

Recipe for a Bog

Block the gullies and grips
        where the river rises,

slow the downhill flow
        of peat-filled streams.

Fell spruce and pine
        that thirst for moisture,

mulch parched earth
        with heather brash.

Graft sphagnum moss
        from a healthy bank,

lay straw,
        feather-light on fragments.

Welcome rain,
        gaze at puddles

spreading into ponds.
        Count frogs.

Watch emperor moths
        in cotton grass,

a spider trapped
        on sundew tendrils,

dragonflies skittish
        from butterwort to asphodel

and a pair of low-flying merlin
        wingbeat, wingbeat, glide.

spawn

all winter they sit still
as little Buddhas

hidden in leaf litter
breathing through their skin

tonight the moon is full
snow melt swells the stream

they gather at the ragged pond
yellow olive green and bronze

clasp tight with nuptial pads
and set the water rocking

among forget-me-nots
marsh marigolds and mint

a double bass octet
they yield a trove

At Purteen Harbour

Basking sharks, docile as seal pups,
harpooned and netted from currachs,

were towed one by one to the fishery
at the slipway. Fathers and sons

sliced off dorsal fins and hacked
through blubber to reach oil-filled livers.

Sweating in burn-house heat,
they shovelled bleeding flesh

into the rendering machine.
They couldn't wash the smell

from their skin, not if they swam
to Inis Gealbhan at the end of every shift.

Year by year the catch diminished,
disappeared.

But late last April, old men
cheered from the headland, and said

It's as if we've been forgiven –
a school of twelve cruised into Keem Bay,

moon tails swishing, fins proud
as yawl sails above the waves.

Little Tern Colony, Kilcoole

In shallow nests among pebbles
most of the eggs survived the high tides.

August slips into September. Fledglings,
light as whelk shells, get ready to fly.

The sun and stars will guide them,
and though they'll be hungry, thirsty, cold,

the earth's magnetic field
will pulse in their hearts like hope.

Mater Misericordiae

Still new to each other
when you found the lump,

we held our breath as the surgeon
marked the spot with an X.

A porter pushed your trolley
down the echoing corridor –

I stayed at the edge of your bed.
The matron asked was I a relation

and under the Sacred Heart lamp
I called myself a friend.

Later I searched for coins
and a pay phone

to tell your mother
you were back in the ward,

sleepy but smiling.
The rose-petal scar on your breast

was tiny, but enough to remind us
we'd already found what mattered.

The Key

The house looked like home that evening in May:
honeysuckle tangled in hazel,

oak breaking into leaf, the kitchen warmed
by a stove. Windows praised the hills.

It rains the day we're handed the key –
linoleum curling in corners,

damp patches on ceilings, blinds we can't raise.
A marble rolls in an empty drawer.

Heads down, eyes not meeting,
we turn up the radio, sweep and scrub,

unpack boxes, place our books on shelves.
Darkness tells us it's time to rest.

Lifting the bedside lamp from the car,
we hear the Avonbeg at the end of the road,

smell hay in our neighbour's field.
A horse whinnies. Venus unlocks the sky.

Spalls

To help us grow a garden, my mother and father travelled
across the Bog of Allen and over the Wicklow Gap.

They'd have preferred to drive west to Galway or Mayo,
they'd have preferred a husband and children

but their daughter loved a woman. We'd have the table set
for breakfast: rashers, black pudding, fried bread and eggs.

When the soil had warmed, we unloaded shovels
and rakes, buckets of compost and the rusted iron bar

for prising out rocks. The back seat was thronged
with pots of seedlings my mother had nurtured all winter.

We worked to her bidding: *loosen tangled roots before planting,
sow marigolds next to beans, sprinkle Epsom salts around roses.*

My father took off on his own to spud ragwort or clip a hedge.
One day he spent hours gathering stones of different shapes and sizes.

By evening he'd built us a wall under the holly, held together
by gravity and friction, hearted with handfuls of spalls.

Her first

The sun tries to shine
through narrow frosted windows,

while we wait with the other births,
deaths and marriages.

Close to lunchtime
the registrar ushers us into her office;

stacks of files on every surface
look set to topple.

She murmurs *You're my first*,
and reads out the regulations,

then shuffles through papers,
studies the stapler on her desk

and reads them again.
When we tell her

we've been together twenty years
she stops searching for a biro,

meets our eyes and smiles
It'll be a beautiful day.

Wife

Strange to use this word
for the woman I love –

is she my wife
when she lays her head on my shoulder,

when I whisper her name
in the morning to see if she's awake,

or when we plant bluebells
under the oak

where we buried one dog, three cats
and a handful of dreams?

I practise saying *Isobel is my wife*
and it sings to the tune of my life.

Ballinabarney

Gorse thrives in our almost-acre
   on the windward side of a hill –

soil acidic as lemon,
   stones embedded in every inch.

Neighbours tell us nettles
   are a sign of a fertile tilth.

Damselflies rest on a rickety fence
   that hinders cows and sheep.

Oaks throw acorns into gravel
   for saplings to root next spring.

A hedgehog builds her hoglet nest
   in the compost heap, swallows

own the shed. A fox crosses the lawn,
   nonchalant bronze on his journey

to somewhere else. Jays
   chase siskins from feeders

while brambles slither
   unstoppable from every ditch

and, in our unmown corners, dandelions,
   knapweed and thistles persist.

First Earlies

By rights we'd be standing side by side,
making idle conversation as we wait

to shake hands with our grieving neighbours
after Requiem Mass in Greenan,

but we keep the byroad between us today.
The virus lingers, a low-lying cloud,

until someone asks about planting first earlies.
Advice flies from gateway to gateway:

you can split seed potatoes
as long as each half has a chit;

dig plenty of manure into the drill,
place them a foot apart, a fist deep;

don't forget to earth up the shoots,
they'll be ready for lifting mid-June.

Sharpe's Express, Setanta, Orla,
Slaney, Red Cara, Accord...

our litany's only hushed
by the hearse coming down the road.

Shepherd

When he was a boy these upland fields
grew more gorse and rushes than grass.
He dug up rocks, shifted stones

to ditches and laneways, ploughed
hummocks into the ground, harrowed
furrows, seeded tilth.

We'd meet him on our way up Kirikee –
crouched to a ewe on her rump,
he'd be clearing thorns from sore hooves

before trimming. He'd pause to lament
harsh weather or laugh at lambs
nudging each other from hillocks.

Was it last year we first saw him
sit for a breath, his collie
resting her head on his knee?

On a midwinter morning,
neighbours line the length of road
downhill to the church at Ballinatone.

Ewes huddle close in lambing sheds
and through the five-bar gate to the yard
an easterly wind keens silver.

Fences

Lights flicker on in houses
        scattered along the byroad –

one of our neighbours
        will be calling children for dinner,

another will be locking in hens,
        closing a rain-swollen door

and heeling off her wellingtons.
        Gorse hedges give shelter,

barbed wire keeps sheep from wandering,
        but what makes good neighbours

is the search for the cat gone missing,
        the loan of a pickaxe,

a push downhill
        for the car that won't start, or,

when snow lies frozen in three-foot drifts,
        the currant bread left on a doorstep.

Thief in April

A red squirrel's stretched
   upside down from a branch

in the rowan
   to the blue tit feeder.

      A tentative step –

he zips back
   and sits upright,

haloed in sunrise
   from ear tufts to fluffed-out tail.

      Half a step –

and he's gone,
   needle-nimble

down the trunk,
   across frosted grass.

      Wild as the morning –

he spirals
   up the holly

and springs,
   windblown limb to limb.

Stepping in

Rain stipples the river
as you huddle for shelter,

balancing on one foot to undress,
then clamber over the fence

for the down-the-bank scramble
through cattails and hazel.

Bone-cold awakening of skin –
you ask yourself why

though your body remembers
in every cell;

lemon-mossed pebbles,
damselflies glancing

on brooklime and alder,
scent of the bog from above Glendasan,

and the current that takes you,
alert, electric, alive.

June

Because wild rose fills the garden
        to the sultry-scented brim

and hawkmoths flock to fuchsia
        humming a wordless hymn.

Because pipistrelles flicker past
        heartbeats on the wing

and tonight's the eve of your birthday,
        the air warm as your skin.

Because it's bright till almost midnight
        and the days will be short too soon,

let's stay out here and listen
        for the wood pigeon's five-note tune.

NOTES

Pit Ponies of Glendasan (25–28): Lead was mined in three Wicklow valleys, Glendasan, Glendalough and Glenmalure, from the early 1800s. The last mine closed in 1957, soon after a mining accident in which a local man James Mernagh was killed and his cousin and workmate Robbie Carter was seriously injured. This four-poem sequence was inspired by conversations with Robbie Carter and John Byrne and archived interviews with other former miners. Some of these poems featured in *The Miners' Way*, a poetry documentary produced by Claire Cunningham (Rockfinch Ltd) and broadcast on BBC Radio 4.

All the Way Home (31–40): The sequence responds to the Auerbach family archive of First World War photographs and letters held in the Mary Evans Picture Library, London. Albert Auerbach joined up on the first day of the war, 1st September 1914, and died four years later in the early morning of 1st September 1918. The sequence also honours the 210,000 Irish soldiers who fought and 40,000 who died in World War I. The poems were originally published in the illustrated chapbook, *All the Way Home* (Smith|Doorstop, 2019).

You could say it begins (42–48): The border in Ireland was created in 1921 under the United Kingdom Parliament's Government of Ireland Act 1920. It runs for 310 miles from Lough Foyle in the north of Ireland to Carlingford Lough in the north-east, separating the Republic of Ireland from Northern Ireland. These poems were inspired by conversations with women from diverse communities on both sides of the border, courtesy of the Across the Lines peace-building programme in the Glen Centre, Manorhamilton, Co. Leitrim. Belfast composer Elaine Agnew set the poem 'You could say it begins' to music which was first performed by Sonamus Music Ensemble in the Mermaid Theatre, Co. Wicklow, in March 2022. Detailed geographical mapping in the borderlands website informed the poem: see http://www.irishborderlands.com/project/index.html

Lazy Beds (52): 'Lazy beds', a traditional ridge and furrow method for growing potatoes, was particularly suited to the poor soil of the uplands where remaining ripples can be seen to this day.

Passage (54): 1480 tenants evicted from the Mahon estate at Strokestown Park, Co. Roscommon were escorted on foot by the bailiff to sail from Dublin to Liverpool and from there to Grosse Île, Quebec, in May 1847.

Wildfire (55): In April 2021 a wildfire damaged or destroyed a range of precious habitats over 2000 hectares in Killarney National Park, including ancient oak and other woodlands, wet heath, dry heath, blanket bog, exposed rock vegetation, and Molinia wet grassland.

ACKNOWLEDGEMENTS

As well as the publishers and producer of *All the Way Home* and *The Miners' Way* credited in the preceding Notes, I wish to thank the editors of the following publications where several of the poems in this book first appeared: *The Irish Times*; *Poetry Ireland Review*; *The North*; *Banshee*; *Rattle*; *Irish Wildlife*; *One for Everyone: More Poems I Love*, compiled by Kathleen Watkins (Gill Books, 2020); *Roundwood & District Historical, Folklore & Archaeological Society No. 29* (2020); *WRITE Where We Are NOW* (Manchester Metropolitan University blog, 2020); *Days of Clear Light*, edited by Nessa O'Mahony & Alan Hayes (Salmon Poetry, 2021); *Divining Dante*, edited by Nessa O'Mahony & Paul Munden (Recent Work Press, 2021); *Dream of the River*, edited by Natalie Eleanor Patterson (Jacar Press, 2021); *Empty House*, edited by Alice Kinsella & Nessa O'Mahony (Doire Press 2021); *Local Wonders: Poems of our Immediate Surrounds*, edited by Pat Boran (Dedalus Press, 2021); *Queering the Green*, edited by Paul Maddern (Lifeboat Press, 2021); Richard Nairn: *Wild Shores: The Magic of Ireland's Coastline* (Gill Books, 2022); Richard Nairn: *Wild Waters: The Magic of Ireland's Rivers and Lakes* (Gill Books, 2023); *Chasing Shadows*, edited by Noel Monahan (Creative Ireland, 2022).

My thanks also to RTÉ Television's *Nationwide*, RTÉ Radio One's *Countrywide*, *Sunday Miscellany*, *Arena*, *Nature Nights* and *The Poetry Programme*, RTÉ Lyric FM's *Poetry File*, and the *Words Lightly Spoken* podcast, where several of these poems were first broadcast.

I acknowledge with gratitude the Ireland Chair of Poetry Travel Award 2022. I also wish to gratefully acknowledge the Arts Council of Ireland for the award of a Literature Bursary and an Agility Award in 2021. Wicklow County Council Arts Office, Heritage Office and Library Service have provided invaluable support for my work on this collection as well as previous publications. My thanks to the Heinrich Böll Committee for a generative residency on Achill Island in September 2020.

My gratitude for the following inspiring commissions: 'Eggs' – 2021 Festival in a Van & Poetry Ireland Words Move tour; 'You could say it begins' – Sonamus Music Ensemble, marking the hundredth anniversary of the establishment of the border in Ireland, as part of the Decade of Centenaries Commemorations 2021; 'The Dipper', 'Lazy Beds', 'skein', 'Recipe for a Bog', 'Refuge' and 'Stepping in' – County Wicklow Arts & Heritage Offices Avonmore River Project; 'Passage' – Vincent Woods & Edwina Guckian for the 2021 Strokestown International Poetry Festival film, *Bealach an Fhéir Gortaigh, Hunger's Way*; 'Little Tern Colony, Kilcoole' – RTE One Television for SHINE: Summer Concert & Illuminations, August 2020; 'Shepherd' – The Royal Irish Academy podcaster-in-residence Zoë Comyns for Shelfmarks, a podcast looking at Irish nature writing, broadcast in October 2021.

Heartfelt thanks to my editor Neil Astley and also Christine Macgregor and everyone at Bloodaxe Books for their invaluable support and their dedication to poets and poetry.

Thanks to the musicians with whom I have had the pleasure of performing many of these poems: Eamon Sweeney, Cormac Breathnach, Rachel Factor and Annette Cleary of Sonamus Music Ensemble and the piper James Mahon. My gratitude to composer Elaine Agnew for her evocative setting of 'You could say it begins'.

I am deeply grateful to the many people who have helped me develop my work, particularly my long-time companions in poetry Eithne Hand, Jessica Traynor, Rosamund Taylor, Stuart Pickford and Geraldine Mitchell. Also thanks to Moniza Alvi, John Glenday, Eina McHugh, Mary Ryan, Andrew Clarke, Catherine Phil McCarthy, Nessa O'Mahony, Claire Cunningham, Carmel O'Toole, Robbie Carter, James Rebanks, Richard Nairn, Helen Lawless & Mairead Kennedy, Paddy Woodworth, Paddy & Darlene Meskell, Fran & Dave O'Grady, Irini Tendall, and the McMullen family. My gratitude to poet Gillian Clarke who so generously helped me lay the foundations.

Many thanks to my family, friends and neighbours, my mother Dora Clarke, my late father Charlie Clarke and my first reader Isobel O'Duffy.